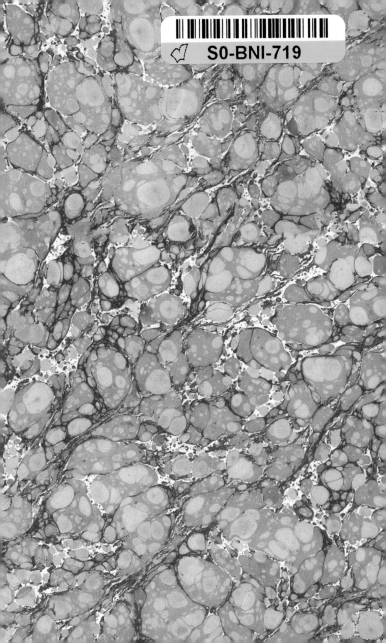
S0-BNI-719

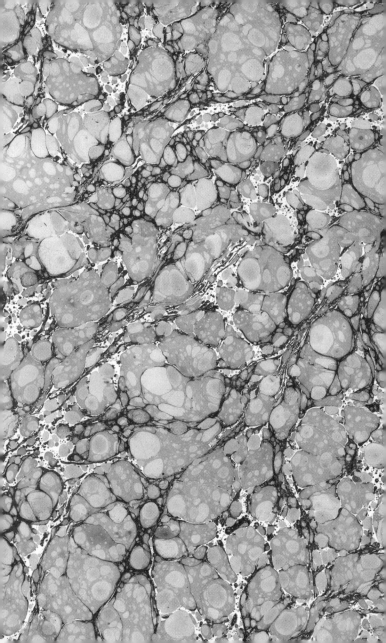

SIR WALTER'S VERSE

SIR WALTER'S
VERSE

A Selection of Scott's Poetry

SELECTED
& INTRODUCED BY

ERIC ANDERSON

THE
ABBOTSFORD
PRESS
2013

This collection
first published in 2013 by
THE ABBOTSFORD PRESS
Melrose · Roxburghshire · Scotland TD6 9BQ

Designed and typeset in Verdigris by Dalrymple
Printed and bound in Poland by OZGRAF
Map drawn by Neil Gower

ISBN 978 0 9575205 1 6

Cover: Sir Thomas Lawrence (1769–1830)
Portrait of Sir Walter Scott, c.1820 (detail)
© *The Royal Collection Trust / Her Majesty Queen Elizabeth II 2013*

Frontispiece: Augustin Edouart (1789–1861)
Silhouette of Sir Walter Scott, c.1830–1
National Portrait Gallery, London

ABBOTSFORD
THE HOME OF *Sir Walter Scott*

CONTENTS

8   Map

11 Introduction

I · TRADITIONAL VERSE: BALLADS & SONGS

16 Sir Patrick Spens

22 The Wife of Usher's Well

25 The Twa Corbies

27 The Battle of Otterbourne

34 The Douglas Tragedy

38 The Eve of St John

47 Rosabelle

50 The Maid of Neidpath

52 Lochinvar

55 Bonnie Dundee

62 Jock of Hazeldean

II · ROMANCES IN VERSE

66   The Last Minstrel

69   Flodden's Fatal Field

72   The Stag Hunt

76   The Eve of Bannockburn

III · REMINISCENCES IN VERSE

84   The End of Autumn

87   Smailholm Tower

91   Summer Rambles

93   Christmas

IV · SCOTLAND IN VERSE

100   O Caledonia

102   Melrose

103   Norham

104   Tantallon Castle

107   Edinburgh

109   Loch Katrine

V · VERSE FROM THE NOVELS

112   The Spindle Song

113   Sound, sound the Clarion

114   Lucy Ashton's Song

115   Proud Maisie

VI · PERSONAL VERSE

118   The Prisoner's Complaint

121   The Violet

122   On the Roman Wall

123   Woman

— * —

124   Epilogue: William Wordsworth's Farewell

127   Scott's Life

FIRTH of FORTH

NORTH SEA

Tantallon

Lammermuir Hills

Melrose

iestiel

Smailholm

R. Tweed

Norham

× Flodden

Kelso

arrow

× Ancram Moor

ABBOTSFORD

Newark

× Otterburn

Canonbie

Newcastle

Netherby

Gower

INTRODUCTION

IR WALTER SCOTT WAS THE great story-teller of the nineteenth century. His historical novels changed the reading habits of the public and opened the way for the great age of the Victorian novel. But his first tales were in verse and he was a best-selling poet before he was a best-selling novelist.

In 1813 he was invited to become Poet Laureate. As it happens he refused, but it would have been the obvious appointment, since to his own age Walter Scott was Scott the poet. When he wrote his first novel, *Waverley*, in 1814 he published it anonymously in case it failed and damaged his reputation as a poet. Poetry was popular leisure reading in the years immediately before the novel became the dominant literary form, and Scott's, energetic, romantic, historical poems had taken the reading public by storm. *The Lay of the Last Minstrel* (1805), *Marmion* (1808), *The Lady of the Lake*

(1810) and *The Lord of the Isles* (1815) were read by almost everybody who could read.

New-comers to Scott are well-advised to begin with his verse. This little collection includes ballads, songs and personal poetry as well as passages from his great narrative romances. Readers who enjoy this introduction to Scott's verse should not resist the temptation to try *Marmion* or *The Lady of the Lake* next.

I

TRADITIONAL VERSE: BALLADS & SONGS

The first four ballads printed here are strictly speaking not by Scott himself. When he collated different versions of traditional ballads from early manuscript sources and from oral tradition for *The Minstrelsy of the Scottish Border* (1802) his intention was not to find the most scholarly text but to make this vigorous folk poetry accessible for the first time to the reading public. So he was happy to alter and improve. Where there were variant readings his policy was simply to choose 'the best or most poetical'. He inserted verses from one version into another; rearranged lines when that was necessary for the sense or the rhyme, and did not scruple to add words or lines of his own. The poems from *The Minstrelsy* are included here partly because Scott has some claim to part-authorship, but mainly because they were the foundation-stones of the poetic style and poetic world of many of the poems which followed, where he strove:

> *in changeful hue,*
> *Field, feast, and combat to renew,*
> *And loves, and arms, and harpers' glee,*
> *And all the pomp of chivalry.*

The Minstrelsy of the Scottish Border made an instant reputation for Scott. There had been other collections of ballads, such as Percy's *Reliques of Ancient English Poetry* which enthralled Scott as a boy, but we owe a quarter of all our Border Ballads to *The Minstrelsy*. It was a lengthy labour of love. As a young man Scott spent seven vacations trekking into the remoter parts of the Border country, seeking out shepherds and old people who could sing or recite traditional ballads to him. He also had access to three manuscript collections and he encouraged friends to send him both old and imitation ballads.

In *The Minstrelsy* the ballads were arranged under three headings: Historical Ballads, Romantic Ballads and Modern Imitations. The historical ballads have at least some foundation in history; the romantic ballads tell of 'legends and marvellous adventures'; the imitations are by Scott himself and some of his friends.

The dialect is easy to understand once you apply two simple rules — that the standard English 'o' is often replaced by a long 'a' sound, and that final letters are sometimes dropped. So, for example, in the ballads, *faem* means *foam*, and:

a'	*all*	hame	*home*
ane	*one*	mair	*more*
awa'	*away*	mak	*make*
gae	*go*	rade	*rode*
gane	*gone*	sae	*so*
ha'	*hall*	tak	*take*

¶ No-one knows if there was such a person as Sir Patrick Spens. There is no record of him, nor of the drowning of the flower of Scotland's nobility on a mission to Norway. None the less the ballad probably has some foundation in historical fact. Before Alexander III of Scotland died in 1285, it was agreed that the crown would pass to his grand-daughter, the 'Maid of Norway'. A ship may have made an ill-fated voyage to Norway and set off home empty-handed when the king refused to let the Maid go, and the ballad may record that event.

Scott had at least three differing versions of the ballad. Only the one taken from an oral source had the verses about the attempt to stem the leak. The ending posed a problem. One of his manuscript versions had the wonderful lines

'Half-owre, half owre, to Aberdour
'Tis fifty fathoms deep'

and it is surprising that Scott preferred 'O forty miles off Aberdeen'.

When there was an evening of music at Abbotsford Sir Patrick Spens was a ballad Scott sometimes chanted to visitors (he was not much of a singer). One guest reported that he rendered the final two lines very slowly and sonorously.

The king sits in Dumfermline town,
    Drinking the blude-red wine:
'O whare will I get a skeely skipper,   *skilful*
    To sail this new ship of mine?'

O up and spake an eldern knight,
    Sat at the king's right knee:
'Sir Patrick Spens is the best sailor
    That ever sailed the sea.'

Our king has written a braid letter,
    And sealed it with his hand,
And sent it to Sir Patrick Spens,
    Was walking on the strand.

'To Noroway, to Noroway,
    To Noroway o'er the faem;
The king's daughter of Noroway,
    'T is thou maun bring her hame.'

The first word that Sir Patrick read,
    Sae loud, loud laughed he;
The neist word that Sir Patrick read,
    The tear blinded his ee.

'O wha is this has done this deed,
    And tauld the king o' me,
To send us out at this time of the year
    To sail upon the sea?

'Be it wind, be it weet, be it hail, be it sleet,
    Our ship must sail the faem;
The king's daughter of Noroway,
    'T is we must fetch her hame.'

They hoysed their sails on Monenday morn,
    Wi' a' the speed they may;
They hae landed in Noroway,
    Upon a Wodensday.

They hadna been a week, a week
    In Noroway but twae,
When that the lords o' Noroway
    Began aloud to say:

'Ye Scottishmen spend a' our king's goud,
    And a' our queenis fee!'
'Ye lie, ye lie, ye liars loud,
    Fu loud I hear ye lie!

'For I brought as much white monie
    As gane my men and me,   *suffices*
And I brought a half-fou o' gude red goud   *bushel*
    Out o'er the sea wi' me.

Make ready, make ready, my merrymen a',
    Our gude ship sails the morn.'
'Now, ever alack! my master dear,
    I fear a deadly storm!

[18]

'I saw the new moon late yestreen,
    Wi' the auld moon in her arm;
And if we gang to sea, master,
    I fear we'll come to harm.'

They hadna sailed a league, a league,
    A league but barely three,
When the lift grew dark, and the wind blew loud,   *sky*
    And gurly grew the sea.   *stormy*

The ankers brak, and the topmasts lap,
    It was sic a deadly storm,
And the waves came o'er the broken ship,
    Till a' her sides were torn.

'O where will I get a gude sailor,
    To take my helm in hand,
Till I get up to the tall topmast,
    To see if I can spy land?'

'O here am I, a sailor gude,
    To take the helm in hand,
Till you go up to the tall topmast;
    But I fear you'll ne'er spy land.'

He hadna gane a step, a step,
    A step but barely ane,
When a bout flew out of our goodly ship,   *plank*
    And the salt sea it came in.

'Gae fetch a web o' the silken claith,   *cloth*
    Another o' the twine,
And wap them into our ship's side,
    And letna the sea come in.'

They fetched a web o' the silken claith,
    Another o' the twine,
And they wapped them roun that gude ship's side,
    But still the sea came in.

O laith, laith were our gude Scots lords   *loath*
    To weet their cork-heeled shoon;
But lang or a' the play was played,
    They wat their hats aboon.

And mony was the feather-bed
    That flattered on the faem,
And mony was the gude lord's son
    That never mair cam hame.

    The ladies wrang their fingers white,
    The maidens tore their hair,
A' for the sake of their true loves,
    For them they'll see na mair.   *no more*

O lang, lang may the ladies sit,
    Wi their fans into their hand,
Before they see Sir Patrick Spens
    Come sailing to the strand.

And lang, lang may the maidens sit,
    Wi' their goud kaims in their hair,   *gold combs*
A' waiting for their ain dear loves,
    For them they'll see na mair.

O forty miles off Aberdeen
    'T is fifty fathoms deep,
And there lies gude Sir Patrick Spens,
    Wi' the Scots lords at his feet.

— THE WIFE OF USHER'S WELL —

¶ *One of the best-known of the many supernatural ballads.*

There lived a wife at Usher's Well,
  And a wealthy wife was she;
She had three stout and stalwart sons,
  And sent them o'er the sea.

They hadna been a week from her,
  A week but barely ane,
When word came to the carline wife   *old crone*
  That her three sons were gane.

They hadna been a week from her,
  A week but barely three,
Whan word came to the carline wife
  That her sons she'd never see.

—'I wish the wind may never cease,
  Nor fashes in the flood,   *troubles on the sea*
Till my three sons come hame to me,
  In earthly flesh and blood.'—

It fell about the Martinmass,
  When nights are lang and mirk,
The carline wife's three sons came hame,
  And their hats were o' the birk   *wreathed with birch*

It neither grew in syke nor ditch,   *drain*
   Nor yet in ony sheugh;   *marsh*
But at the gates o' paradise,
That birk grew fair enough.

—'Blow up the fire, my maidens;
   Bring water from the well:
For a' my house shall feast this night,
   Since my three sons are well.'—

And she has made to them a bed,
   She's made it large and wide,
And she's ta'en her mantle her about,
   Sat down at the bed-side.

Up then crew the red, red cock,
   And up then crew the gray;
The eldest to the youngest said,
   — ''Tis time we were away.'—

The cock he hadna crawed but once,
   And clapped his wings at a',
When the youngest to the eldest said,
   —'Brother, we must awa'.

[23]

'The cock doth craw, the day doth daw,
    The channerin' worm doth chide;   *fretting*
Gin we be missed out o' our place,
    A sair pain we maun bide.

'Fare ye weel, my mother dear!
    Fareweel to barn and byre!
And fare ye weel, the bonny lass,
    That kindles my mother's fire!'—

— THE TWA CORBIES —

¶ Although similar to the old English ballad of 'The Three Ravens', this is a tale not of loyalty but of murder with a motive. Scott had it from his friend Charles Kirkpatrick Sharpe, who had it from a lady, who wrote it down after hearing it.

As I was walking all alane,
I heard twa corbies making a mane;
The tane unto the t'other say,
'Where sall we gang and dine to-day?'

'In behint yon auld fail dyke,   *old turf wall*
I wot there lies a new slain knight;
And naebody kens that he lies there,
But his hawk, his hound, and lady fair.

'His hound is to the hunting gane,
His hawk to fetch the wild-fowl hame,
His lady's ta'en another mate,
So we may mak our dinner sweet.

'Ye'll sit on his white hause-bane;   *collar-bone*
And I'll pike out his bonny blue een;
Wi'ae lock o' his gowden hair
We'll theek our nest when it grows bare.   *thatch*

'Mony a one for him makes mane,   *moan*
But nane sall ken where he is gane;
O'er his white banes, when they are bare,
The wind sall blaw for evermair.'

¶ *This ballad was Scott's favourite. He often quoted it , and recited from it when showing friends the grave of Douglas in Melrose Abbey.*

In August 1388 James , Earl of Douglas, led a Scottish army over the border. In a skirmish at Newcastle he unhorsed Hotspur (Harry Percy, the son of the Earl of Northumberland) and carried off the pennon from his lance. Hotspur raised an army immediately and surprised the Scots in a night attack on their camp at Otterburn. Douglas was killed; Percy was taken prisoner and ransomed for 7,000 marks.

A memorial stands on the supposed site of the battle , just north-west of the village of Otterburn.

> It fell about the Lammas tide,
>   When the muir-men win their hay,
> The doughty earl of Douglas rode
>   Into England, to catch a prey.
>
> He chose the Gordons and the Graemes,
>   With them the Lindesays, light and gay;
> But the Jardines wald not with him ride,
>   And they rue it to this day.

And he has burned the dales of Tyne,
    And part of Bambrough shire;
And three good towers on Reidswire fells,
    He left them all on fire.

And he marched up to Newcastle,
    And rode it round about;
'O wha's the lord of this castle,
    Or wha's the lady o't?'

But up spake proud Lord Percy, then,
    And O but he spake hie!
'I am the lord of this castle,
    My wife's the lady gay.'

'If thou'rt the lord of this castle,
    Sae weel it pleases me!
For ere I cross the border fells
    The tane of us shall die.'

He took a long spear in his hand,
    Shod with the metal free,
And for to meet the Douglas there
    He rode right furiouslie.

But O how pale his lady looked
    Frae aff the castle wa',
When down before the Scottish spear
    She saw proud Percy fa'.

'Had we twa been upon the green,
    And never an eye to see,
I wad hae had you, flesh and fell;
    But your sword shall gae wi' me.'

'But gae ye up to Otterbourne,
    And wait there dayis three;
And if I come not ere three days' end,
A fause knight ca' ye me.'

'The Otterbourne's a bonnie burn;
    'Tis pleasant there to be;
But there is nought at Otterbourne
    To feed my men and me.

The deer rins wild on hill and dale,
    The birds fly wild from tree to tree;
But there is neither bread nor kale
    To fend my men and me.

Yet I will stay at Otterbourne,
    Where you shall welcome be;
And if ye come not at three days' end,
    A fause lord I'll ca' thee,'

'Thither will I come,' proud Percy said,
    By the might of Our Ladye!' -
There will I bide thee,' said the Douglas,
    My trowth I plight to thee.'

They lighted high on Otterbourne,
    Upon the bent sae brown;
They lighted high on Otterbourne,
    And threw their pallions down.

And he that had a bonnie boy,
    Sent out his horse to grass;
And he that had not a bonnie boy,
    His ain servant he was.

But up then spake a little page,
    Before the peep of dawn —
'O waken ye, waken ye, my good lord,
    For Percy's hard at hand.'

'Ye lie, ye lie, ye liar loud!
    Sae loud I hear ye lie :
For Percy had not men yestreen ,
    To dight my men and me.   *cope with*

But I hae dreamed a dreary dream,
    Beyond the Isle of Sky;
I saw a dead man win a fight,
    And I think that man was I.'

He belted on his good braid sword,
    And to the field he ran;
But he forgot the helmet good,
    That should have kept his brain.

When Percy wi' the Douglas met,
   I wat he was fu' fain!
They swakked their swords, till sair they swat,
   And the blood ran down like rain.

But Percy with his good broad sword,
   That could so sharply wound,
Has wounded Douglas on the brow,
   Till he fell to the ground.

Then he called on his little foot-page,
   And said — 'Run speedily,
And fetch my ain dear sister's son,
   Sir Hugh Montgomery.'

'My nephew good,' the Douglas said,
   'What recks the death of ane!
Last night I dreamed a dreary dream,
   And I ken the day's thy ain.

My wound is deep; I fain would sleep;
   Take thou the vanguard of the three,
And hide me by the braken bush,
   That grows on yonder lily lee.

O bury me by the braken bush,
   Beneath the blooming briar,
Let never living mortal ken
   That ere a kindly Scot lies here.'

He lifted up that noble lord,
    Wi' the saut tear in his e'e;
He hid him in the braken bush,
    That his merrie men might not see.

The moon was clear, the day drew near,
    The spears in flinders flew,
But many a gallant Englishman
    Ere day the Scotsmen slew.

The Gordons good in English blood
    They steeped their hose and shoon;
The Lindsays flew like fire about,
    Till all the fray was done.

The Percy and Montgomery met,
    That either of other were fain;
They swapped swords, and they twa swat,
    And aye the blude ran down between.

'Yield thee, O yield thee, Percy!' he said,
    'Or else I vow I'll lay thee low!'
'Whom to shall I yield,' said Earl Percy,
    Now that I see it must be so?'

'Thou shalt not yield to lord nor loun,
    Nor yet shalt thou yield to me;
But yield thee to the braken bush,
    That grows upon yon lily lee!'

'I will not yield to a braken bush,
  Nor yet will I yield to a briar;
But I would yield to Lord Douglas,
  Or Sir Hugh the Montgomery, if he were here.'

As soon as he knew it was Montgomery,
  He struck his sword's point in the gronde;
And the Montgomery was a courteous knight,
  And quickly took him by the honde.

This deed was done at Otterbourne,
  About the breaking of the day;
Earl Douglas was buried at the braken bush,
  And the Percy led captive away.

¶ 'Popular tradition', wrote Scott, 'has pointed out the scene of this fatal story and assigned it to Blackhouse in Selkirkshire where there are ruins of a very ancient castle said to have belonged to Lord William Douglas. The scenery around it is savage and desolate: a stream called the Douglas-Burn is said to have been that where the lovers stopped to drink, and seven huge stones are averred to have been erected in memory of the seven brothers.'

Scott owed this ballad, too, to his friend Charles Kirkpatrick Sharpe but added the last three verses from another version. He particularly liked the last stanza: plants which twined together from two lovers' graves are commonplace in such ballads but the violent anger of the Black Douglas makes these verses memorable. This was a ballad Scott liked to recite on expeditions from Abbotsford.

'Rise up, rise up, now, Lord Douglas,' she says,
    'And put on your armour so bright;
Let it never be said that a daughter of thine
    Was married to a lord under night.

'Rise up, rise up, my seven bold sons,
    And put on your armour so bright,
And take better care of your youngest sister,
    For your eldest's awa' the last night.'

He's mounted her on a milk-white steed,
    And himself on a dapple grey,
With a bugelet horn hung down by his side,
    And lightly they rode away.

Lord William lookit o'er his left shoulder,
    To see what he could see,
And there he spied her seven brethren bold,
    Come riding over the lee.

'Light down, light down, Lady Margret,' he said,
    'And hold my steed in your hand,
Until that against your seven brethren bold,
    And your father, I mak a stand.'

She held his steed in her milk-white hand,
    And never shed one tear,
Until that she saw her seven brethren fa',
    And her father hard fighting, who loved her so dear.

'O hold your hand, Lord William!' she said,
    'For your strokes they are wondrous sair;
True lovers I can get many a ane,
    But a father I can never get mair.'

O she's ta'en out her handkerchief,
    It was o' the holland sae fine,
And aye she dighted her father's bloody wounds,   *wiped*
    That were redder than the wine.

[35]

'O chuse, O chuse, Lady Margret,' he said,
    'O whether will ye gang or bide?'
'I'll gang, I'll gang, Lord William,' she said,
    'For ye have left me no other guide.'

He's lifted her on a milk-white steed,
    And himself on a dapple grey,
With a bugelet horn hung down by his side,
    And slowly they baith rade away.

O they rade on, and on they rade,
    And a' by the light of the moon,
Until they came to yon wan water,
    And there they lighted down.

They lighted down to tak a drink
    Of the spring that ran sae clear,
And down the stream ran his gude heart's blood,
    And sair she gan to fear.

'Hold up, hold up, Lord William,' she says,
    For I fear that you are slain;'
''T is naething but the shadow of my scarlet cloak,
    That shines in the water sae plain.'

O they rade on, and on they rade,
    And a' by the light of the moon,
Until they cam to his mother's ha' door,
    And there they lighted down.

'Get up, get up, lady mother,' he says,
    'Get up, and let me in!
Get up, get up, lady mother,' he says,
    'For this night my fair lady I've win.

O mak my bed, lady mother,' he says,
    'O mak it braid and deep,
And lay Lady Margret close at my back,
    And the sounder I will sleep.'

Lord William was dead lang ere midnight,
    Lady Margret lang ere day,
And all true lovers that go thegither,
    May they have mair luck than they!

Lord William was buried in Saint Mary's kirk,
    Lady Margret in Mary's quire;
Out o' the lady's grave grew a bonny red rose,
    And out o' the knight's a briar.

And they twa met, and they twa plat,
    And fain they wad be near;
And a' the warld might ken right weel
    They were twa lovers dear.

But bye and rade the Black Douglas,
    And wow but he was rough!
For he pulled up the bonny briar,
    And flang't in Saint Mary's Loch.

⁋ *Set at Smailholm, the ruined tower on a craggy hillock beside his grandfather's farm in the Borders, this ballad is all Scott's own. He had loved Smailholm since his childhood, much of which he spent with his grandparents. It was here that his imagination was first fired by hearing the legends and ballads of the Border country.*

In 1798 he persuaded the owner, Hugh Scott of Harden, to undertake some repairs to the old tower. His kinsman asked for a ballad in return. This grim tale of a faithless wife, her lover murdered by her husband and a supernatural visitation was the result.

The battle of Ancram Moor, referred to in the poem, took place in 1545. An English force under Lord Evers was defeated there by Archibald Douglas, Earl of Angus, and by one of Scott's ancestors, 'the bold Buccleuch'.

The Baron of Smailholm rose with day:
    He spurred his courser on,
Without stop or stay, down the rocky way
    That leads to Brotherstone.

He went not with the bold Buccleuch,
    His banner broad to rear;
He went not 'gainst the English yew,
    To lift the Scottish spear.

Yet his plate-jack was braced,   *coat-armour*
          and his helmet was laced,
   And his vaunt-brace of proof he wore;   *shoulder-armour*
At his saddle-gerthe was a good steel sperthe,   *battle-axe*
   Full ten pound weight and more.

The baron returned in three days' space,
   And his looks were sad and sour;
And weary was his courser's pace,
   As he reached his rocky tower.

He came not from where Ancram Moor
   Ran red with English blood;
Where the Douglas true, and the bold Buccleuch,
   'Gainst keen Lord Evers stood.

Yet was his helmet hacked and hewed,
   His acton pierced and tore;   *padded jacket*
His axe and his dagger with blood embrued,
   But it was not English gore.

He lighted at the Chapellage,
   He held him close and still;
And he whistled thrice for his little foot page,
   His name was English Will.

— 'Come thou hither, my little foot-page;
   Come hither to my knee;
Though thou art young, and tender of age,
   I think thou art true to me.

Come, tell me all that thou hast seen;
    And look thou tell me true!
Since I from Smailholm tower have been,
    What did thy lady do?'—

—'My lady, each night, sought the lonely light,
    That burns on the wild Watchfold;
For, from height to height, the beacons bright
    Of the English foemen told.

The bittern clamoured from the moss,
    The wind blew loud and shrill;
Yet the craggy pathway she did cross,
    To the eiry beacon hill.

I watched her steps, and silent came
    Where she sat her on a stone;
No watchman stood by the dreary flame;
    It burned all alone.

The second night I kept her in sight,
    Till to the fire she came,
And, by Mary's might, an armed knight,
    Stood by the lonely flame.

And many a word that warlike lord
    Did speak to my lady there;
But the rain fell fast, and loud blew the blast,
    And I heard not what they were.

The third night there the sky was fair,
    And the mountain blast was still,
As again I watched the secret pair,
    On the lonesome beacon hill.

And I heard her name the midnight hour,
    And name this holy eve;
And say, "Come this night to thy lady's bower;
    Ask no bold Baron's leave.

He lifts his spear with the bold Buccleuch;
    His lady is all alone;
The door she'll undo to her knight so true,
    On the eve of good Saint John."

—"I cannot come; I must not come;
    I dare not come to thee;
On the eve of Saint John I must wander alone:
    In thy bower I may not be."

—"Now, out on thee, faint-hearted knight!
    Thou should'st not say me nay;
For the eve is sweet, and when lovers meet,
    Is worth the whole summer's day.

And I'll chain the blood-hound, and the warder shall not sound,
    And rushes shall be strewed on the stair;
So, by the black rood-stone, and by holy St John,
    I conjure thee, my love, to be there!"—

—"Though the blood-hound be mute, and the rush beneath my foot,
     And the warder his bugle should not blow,
Yet there sleepeth a priest in the chamber to the east,
     And my foot-step he would know."—

—"O fear not the priest, who sleepeth to the east!
     For to Dryburgh the way he has ta'en;
And there to say mass, till three days do pass,
     For the soul of a knight that is slain."—

He turned him around, and grimly he frowned;
     Then he laughed right scornfully
—"He who says the mass-rite for the soul of that knight,
     May as well say mass for me.

At the lone midnight hour, when bad spirits have power,
     In thy chamber will I be."—
With that he was gone, and my lady left alone,
     And no more did I see.' —

Then changed, I trow, was that bold Baron's brow,
     From the dark to the blood-red high;
— 'Now tell me the mien of the knight thou hast seen,
     For, by Mary, he shall die!' —

—'His arms shone full bright, in the beacon's red light;
     His plume it was scarlet and blue;
On his shield was a hound, in a silver leash bound,
     And his crest was a branch of the yew.'—

—'Thou liest, thou liest, thou little foot-page,
    Loud dost thou lie to me!
For that knight is cold, and low laid in the mould,
    All under the Eildon tree.'—

—'Yet hear but my word, my noble lord!
    For I heard her name his name;
And that lady bright, she called the knight,
    Sir Richard of Coldinghame.'—

The bold Baron's brow then changed, I trow,
    From high blood-red to pale —
—'The grave is deep and dark, and the corpse is stiff and stark,
    So I may not trust thy tale.

Where fair Tweed flows round holy Melrose,
    And Eildon slopes to the plain,
Full three nights ago, by some secret foe,
    That gay gallant was slain.

The varying light deceived thy sight,
    And the wild winds drowned the name;
For the Dryburgh bells ring, and the white monks do sing,
    For Sir Richard of Coldinghame!'—

He passed the court-gate, and he oped the tower grate,
    And he mounted the narrow stair,
To the bartizan-seat, where, with maids that on her wait,
    He found his lady fair.

That lady sat in mournful mood;
    Looked over hill and vale:
Over Tweed's fair flood, and Mertoun's wood,
    And all down Teviotdale.

—'Now hail! now hail! thou lady bright!'—
    —'Now, hail, thou Baron true!
What news, what news, from Ancram fight?
    What news from the bold Buccleuch?'—

—'The Ancram Moor is red with gore,
    For many a southern fell;
And Buccleuch has charged us, evermore,
    To watch our beacons well.'—

The lady blushed red, but nothing she said;
    Nor added the Baron a word:
Then she stepped down the stair to her chamber fair,
    And so did her moody lord.

In sleep the lady mourned and the Baron tossed and turned,
    And oft to himself he said
—'The worms around him creep, and his bloody grave is deep:
    It cannot give up the dead!'—

It was near the ringing of matin-bell,
    The night was well nigh done,
When a heavy sleep on that Baron fell,
    On the eve of good St John.

The lady looked through the chamber fair,
    By the light of a dying flame;
And she was aware of a knight stood there —
    Sir Richard of Coldinghame!

—'Alas! Away! away!' she cried,
    'For the holy Virgin's sake!'—
—'Lady, I know who sleeps by thy side;
    But, lady, he will not awake.

By Eildon-tree, for long nights three,
    In bloody grave have I lain;
The mass and the death-prayer are said for me,
    But, Lady, they are said in vain.

By the Baron's brand, near Tweed's fair strand,
    Most foully slain I fell;
And my restless sprite on the beacon's height,
    For a space is doomed to dwell.

At our trysting-place, for a certain space,
    I must wander to and fro;
But I had not had power to come to thy bower,
    Had'st thou not conjured me so.'—

Love mastered fear — her brow she crossed;
    —'How, Richard, hast thou sped?
And art thou saved, or art thou lost?'—
    The vision shook his head!

—'Who spilleth life, shall forfeit life;
    So bid thy lord believe:
That lawless love is guilt above,
    This awful sign receive.'—

He laid his left hand on an oaken stand,
    His right hand on her arm:
The lady shrunk, and fainting sunk,
    For the touch was fiery warm.

The sable score of fingers four
    Remains on that board impressed;
And for evermore that lady wore
    A covering on her wrist.

There is a nun in Dryburgh bower,
    Ne'er looks upon the sun:
There is a monk in Melrose tower,
    He speaketh word to none.

That nun, who ne'er beholds the day,
    That monk, who speaks to none —
That nun was Smailholm's Lady gay,
    That Monk the bold Baron.

— ROSABELLE —

¶ Scott's romantic ballad about Rosabelle Saint Clair, who is tempted by love to sail home across the Firth of Forth in a storm, comes from his first great narrative poem, The Lay of the Last Minstrel.

A visit to the wooded glen on the banks of the river Esk, surmounted by Roslin Castle and Roslin Chapel, was a favourite excursion of Scott's from Edinburgh.

> O listen, listen, ladies gay!
> No haughty feat of arms I tell;
> Soft is the note, and sad the lay
> That mourns the lovely Rosabelle.
>
> 'Moor, moor the barge, ye gallant crew!
> And, gentle lady, deign to stay!
> Rest thee in Castle Ravensheuch,
> Nor tempt the stormy firth to-day.
>
> The blackening wave is edged with white;
> To inch and rock the sea-mews fly;
> The fishers have heard the Water-Sprite,
> Whose screams forebode that wreck is nigh.

Last night the gifted Seer did view
A wet shroud swathed round lady gay;
Then stay thee, Fair, in Ravenscheuch;
Why cross the gloomy firth to-day?'

'Tis not because Lord Lindesay's heir
Tonight at Roslin leads the ball,
But that my lady-mother there
Sits lonely in her castle-hall.

'Tis not because the ring they ride,
And Lindesay at the ring rides well,
But that my sire the wine will chide
If 'tis not filled by Rosabelle.'

—O'er Roslin all that dreary night
A wondrous blaze was seen to gleam;
'Twas broader than the watch-fire's light,
And redder than the bright moonbeam.

It glared on Roslin's castled rock,
It ruddied all the copse-wood glen;
'Twas seen from Dryden's groves of oak,
And seen from caverned Hawthornden.

Seemed all on fire that chapel proud
Where Roslin's chiefs uncoffined lie,
Each Baron, for a sable shroud,
Sheathed in his iron panoply.

Seemed all on fire within, around,
Deep sacristy and altar's pale;
Shone every pillar foliage-bound,
And glimmered all the dead men's mail.

Blazed battlement and pinnet high, *banner*
Blazed every rose-carved buttress fair —
So still they blaze, when fate is nigh
The lordly line of high Saint Clair.

There are twenty of Roslin's barons bold
Lie buried within that proud chapelle;
Each one the holy vault doth hold
But the sea holds lovely Rosabelle!

And each Saint Clair was buried there
With candle, with book, and with knell;
But the sea-caves rung, and the wild winds sung
The dirge of lovely Rosabelle.

— THE MAID OF NEIDPATH —

¶ *Neidpath Castle, near Peebles, was said to be haunted by the ghost of Jean Douglas. Forbidden by her father to marry the man she loved, she pined away so much that her lover failed to recognize her when he returned to claim her. Visiting the castle in 1803 Wordsworth was as outraged as Scott that the owner had chopped down part of the avenue of trees and wrote a sonnet beginning 'Degenerate Douglas! Oh the unworthy lord.'*

O lovers' eyes are sharp to see,
  And lovers' ears in hearing;
And love, in life's extremity,
  Can lend an hour of cheering.
Disease had been in Mary's bower
  And slow decay from mourning,
Though now she sits on Neidpath's tower
  To watch her Love's returning.

All sunk and dim her eyes so bright,
  Her form decayed by pining,
Till through her wasted hand, at night,
  You saw the taper shining.
By fits a sultry hectic hue
  Across her cheek was flying;
By fits so ashy pale she grew
  Her maidens thought her dying.

[50]

Yet keenest powers to see and hear
    Seemed in her frame residing;
Before the watch-dog pricked his ear
    She heard her lover's riding;
Ere scarce a distant form was kenned
    She knew and waved to greet him,
And o'er the battlement did bend
    As on the wing to meet him.

He came — he passed — an heedless gaze
    As o'er some stranger glancing:
Her welcome, spoke in faltering phrase,
    Lost in his courser's prancing —
The castle-arch, whose hollow tone
    Returns each whisper spoken,
Could scarcely catch the feeble moan
    Which told her heart was broken.

— LOCHINVAR —

¶ *One of Scott's own favourites, 'Lochinvar' was originally written for Lady Dalkeith and then included in* Marmion. *When bringing his own wife to Scotland, Scott had less obstacles to overcome than his imaginary hero, but he courted her at Gilsland, only a few miles from the places named in the poem, and after their wedding in Carlisle brought her home over the Border by way of Netherby and Canonbie.*

O young Lochinvar is come out of the west,
Through all the wide Border his steed was the best;
And save his good broadsword he weapons had none,
He rode all unarmed, and he rode all alone.
So faithful in love, and so dauntless in war,
There never was knight like the young Lochinvar.

He stayed not for brake, and he stopped not for stone,
He swam the Esk river where ford there was none;
But ere he alighted at Netherby gate,
The bride had consented, the gallant came late:
For a laggard in love, and a dastard in war,
Was to wed the fair Ellen of brave Lochinvar.

So boldly he entered the Netherby Hall,
Among bride's-men, and kinsmen, and brothers and all:
Then spoke the bride's father, his hand on his sword,
(For the poor craven bridegroom said never a word),
'O come ye in peace here, or come ye in war,
Or to dance at our bridal, young Lord Lochinvar?'

'I long wooed your daughter, my suit you denied; —
Love swells like the Solway, but ebbs like its tide —
And now I am come, with this lost love of mine,
To lead but one measure, drink one cup of wine.
There are maidens in Scotland more lovely by far,
That would gladly be bride to the young Lochinvar.'

The bride kissed the goblet: the knight took it up,
He quaffed off the wine, and he threw down the cup.
She looked down to blush, and she looked up to sigh,
With a smile on her lips and a tear in her eye.
He took her soft hand, ere her mother could bar, —
'Now tread we a measure!' said young Lochinvar.

So stately his form, and so lovely her face,
That never a hall such a galliard did grace;
While her mother did fret, and her father did fume
And the bridegroom stood dangling his bonnet and plume,
And the bride-maidens whispered, ''Twere better by far
To have matched our fair cousin with young Lochinvar.'

One touch to her hand, and one word in her ear,
When they reached the hall-door, and the charger stood near;
So light to the croupe the fair lady he swung,
So light to the saddle before her he sprung!
'She is won! we are gone, over bank, bush, and scaur;
They'll have fleet steeds that follow,' quoth young Lochinvar.

There was mounting 'mong Graemes of the Netherby clan;
Forsters, Fenwicks, and Musgraves, they rode and they ran:
There was racing and chasing on Canonbie Lee,
But the lost bride of Netherby ne'er did they see.

So daring in love, and so dauntless in war,
Have ye e'er heard of gallant like young Lochinvar?

— BONNIE DUNDEE —

¶ *James Graham of Claverhouse, 1st Viscount Dundee, was 'Bloody Claverse' to his enemies and 'Bonnie Dundee' to his royalist friends. Scott thought him a gallant, romantic soldier. He owned a miniature of him and also one of his pistols.*

The Covenanters — Scottish Presbyterians who had signed the National Covenant to protect the independence of the protestant churches — hated Claverhouse and with good reason. When Charles II attempted to impose episcopacy and the Anglican prayer book on Scotland it was Claverhouse who commanded the royalist horse at the battle of Bothwell Bridge and was responsible throughout the 'Killing Time' which followed for hunting down Covenanters, or 'Whigs', throughout the West of Scotland. He was believed to be in league with the devil and to be invulnerable to anything but a silver bullet.

In Old Mortality, *the novel set in that time, Scott has him say:*

'When I think of death as a thing worth thinking of, it is in the hope of pressing one day some well-fought and hard-won field of battle, and dying with the shout of victory in my ear — that would be worth dying for, and more, it would be worth having lived for.'

He had his wish, as he died in the moment of victory at the Battle of Killiecrankie in 1689.

The poem records an incident earlier that year. A Convention of the Estates (in effect the Scottish parliament of the day) met in Edinburgh to consider the conditions on which they would support William of Orange as king. With the debate going against him, Dundee flounced out and set off through Edinburgh to raise an army to fight for the deposed King James.

In his Journal for 22 December 1825 Scott wrote:

> The air of 'Bonnie Dundee' running in my head
> to-day I wrote a few verses to it before dinner,
> taking the key-note from the story of Claverse
> leaving the Scottish Convention of Estates in
> 1688–9. I wonder if they are good.'

Scott's liking for Bonnie Dundee may have been enhanced by pride in his own great-grandfather, who fought alongside him at Killiecrankie. The portrait of this Walter Scott, who was nicknamed 'Beardie' as he resolved never to shave until a Jacobite king came to the throne, hangs in Abbotsford.

To the Lords of Convention 'twas Claver'se who spoke.
'Ere the King's crown shall fall there are crowns to be broke;
So let each Cavalier who loves honour and me,
Come follow the bonnet of Bonnie Dundee.
    Come fill up my cup, come fill up my can,
    Come saddle your horses, and call up your men;
    Come open the West Port and let me gang free
    And it's room for the bonnets of Bonnie Dundee!'

Dundee he is mounted, he rides up the street,
The bells are rung backward, the drums they are beat;
But the Provost, douce man, said, 'Just e'en let him be,
The Gude Town is weel quit of that De'il of Dundee.'
    'Come fill up my cup, come fill up my can,
    Come saddle your horses, and call up your men;
    Come open the West Port and let me gang free,
    And it's room for the bonnets of Bonnie Dundee!'

As he rode down the sanctified bends of the Bow,[1]
Ilk carline was flyting and shaking her pow;[2]
But the young plants of grace they looked couthie and slee,[3]
Thinking luck to thy bonnet, thou Bonnie Dundee!

1. The West Bow curves down from the High Street
   in Edinburgh to the Grassmarket.

2. 'Each old crone was cursing and shaking her head.'

3. 'Pleasant and sly.'

'Come fill up my cup, come fill up my can,
Come saddle your horses, and call up your men;
Come open the West Port and let me gang free,
And it's room for the bonnets of Bonnie Dundee!'

With sour-featured Whigs the Grass-market was crammed,[4]
As if half the West had set tryst[5] to be hanged;
There was spite in each look, there was fear in each e'e,
As they watched for the bonnets of Bonnie Dundee.
  'Come fill up my cup, come fill up my can,
  Come saddle your horses, and call up your men;
  Come open the West Port and let me gang free,
  And it's room for the bonnets of Bonnie Dundee!'

These cowls of Kilmarnock[6] had spits and had spears,
And lang-hafted gullies[7] to kill cavaliers;
But they shrunk to close-heads[8] and the causeway was free,
At the toss of the bonnet of Bonnie Dundee.
  'Come fill up my cup, come fill up my can,
  Come saddle your horses, and call up your men;
  Come open the West Port and let me gang free,
  And it's room for the bonnets of Bonnie Dundee!'

4. The Grassmarket was the site of the gallows.

5. 'Made an appointment'.

6. Whigs and Covenanters from Ayrshire.

7. 'Long-handled knives.'

8. 'Alley-ways'

[58]

He spurred to the foot of the proud Castle rock,
And with the gay Gordon[9] he gallantly spoke;
'Let Mons Meg and her marrows[10] speak twa words or three,
For the love of the bonnet of Bonnie Dundee.
    Come fill up my cup, come fill up my can,
    Come saddle your horses, and call up your men;
    Come open the West Port and let me gang free,
    And it's room for the bonnets of Bonnie Dundee!'

The Gordon demands of him which way he goes —
'Where'er shall direct me the shade of Montrose![11]
Your Grace in short space shall hear tidings of me,
Or that low lies the bonnet of Bonnie Dundee.
    Come fill up my cup, come fill up my can,
    Come saddle your horses, and call up your men;
    Come open the West Port and let me gang free,
    And it's room for the bonnets of Bonnie Dundee!

There are hills beyond Pentland and lands beyond Forth,
If there's lords in the Lowlands, there's chiefs in the North;
There are wild Duniewassals[12] three thousand times three,
Will cry hoigh! for the bonnet of Bonnie Dundee.

9. The Duke of Gordon, Constable of Edinburgh Castle.

10. 'The great cannon and its mates.'

11. James Graham, Marquess of Montrose, Charles I's
    captain-general in Scotland.

12. 'Highland warriors.'

Come fill up my cup, come fill up my can,
Come saddle your horses, and call up your men;
Come open the West Port and let me gang free,
And it's room for the bonnets of Bonnie Dundee!

There's brass on the target of barkened[13] bull-hide;
There's steel in the scabbard that dangles beside;
The brass shall be burnished, the steel shall flash free,
At the toss of the bonnet of Bonnie Dundee.
Come fill up my cup, come fill up my can,
Come saddle your horses, and call up your men;
Come open the West Port and let me gang free,
And it's room for the bonnets of Bonnie Dundee!

Away to the hills, to the caves, to the rocks —
Ere I own an usurper, I'll couch with the fox;
And tremble, false Whigs, in the midst of your glee,
You have not seen the last of my bonnet and me!
Come fill up my cup, come fill up my can,
Come saddle your horses, and call up your men;
Come open the West Port and let me gang free,
And it's room for the bonnets of Bonnie Dundee!'

13. 'Tanned'

He waved his proud hand, the trumpets were blown,
The kettle-drums clashed and the horsemen rode on,
Till on Ravelston's cliffs and on Clermiston's lee
Died away the wild war-notes of Bonnie Dundee.
    'Come fill up my cup, come fill up my can,
    Come saddle the horses, and call up the men;
    Come open your gates, and let me gae free,
    For it's up with the bonnets of Bonnie Dundee!'

❡ *The first stanza, which Scott heard sung in 1816, was all that remained of a traditional song. He added three further verses for his daughter Sophia to sing to her harp. When an Italian diva performed the complete version as a compliment to Scott at a concert in Edinburgh, Scott declared privately that his daughter sang it better.*

'Why weep ye by the tide, ladie?
    Why weep ye by the tide?
I'll wed ye to my youngest son,
    And ye sall be his bride:
And ye sall be his bride, ladie,
    Sae comely to be seen' —
But aye she loot the tears down fa'
    For Jock of Hazeldean.

'Now let this wilfu' grief be done,
    And dry that cheek so pale;
Young Frank is chief of Errington,
    And lord of Langley-dale;
His step is first in peaceful ha'
    His sword in battle keen' —
But aye she loot the tears down fa'
    For Jock of Hazeldean.

'A chain of gold you sall not lack,
    Nor braid to bind your hair;
Nor mettled hound, nor managed hawk,
    Nor palfrey fresh and fair;
And you, the foremost o' them a',
    Shall ride our forest queen' —
But aye she loot the tears down fa'
    For Jock of Hazeldean.

The kirk was decked at morning-tide,
    The tapers glimmered fair;
The priest and bridegroom wait the bride,
    And dame and knight are there.
They sought her baith by bower and ha';
    The ladie was not seen!
She's o'er the Border and awa'
    Wi' Jock of Hazeldean.

II

In the early eighteen hundreds when the novel was still in its infancy, Scott's great narrative poems were the universal leisure reading. It is hard to exaggerate their popularity. In an age when 1000 copies represented a good sale, the numbers called for were without parallel up to that time. *The Lay of the Last Minstrel* sold 27,000 copies in ten years, and its success was far exceeded by *The Lady of the Lake*, the publishing sensation of 1810, which sold 25,000 within eight months. That poem had a dramatic effect too on visits to Loch Katrine, the 'lake' of the poem. A friend reported to Scott that 297 carriages had been counted in five months, when the usual annual total was less than a hundred.

Marmion: A Tale of Flodden Field and *The Lord of the Isles*, by mingling fiction and history in the way that the Waverley Novels were to do a few years later, paved the way for the popularity of the historical novel.

These passages give some idea of what attracted the reading public of Scott's day.

— THE LAST MINSTREL —

from *The Lay of the Last Minstrel*

¶ *This 'romance of Border Chivalry and enchantment' — a stirring story of conflict, a goblin and a wizard is put into the mouth of the aged minstrel described in the poem's Introduction below. 'The last of all the bards was he, who sung of Border chivalry' — the last until Scott arrived, that is.*

The way was long, the wind was cold,
The Minstrel was infirm and old;
His withered cheek, and tresses gray,
Seemed to have known a better day;
The harp, his sole remaining joy,
Was carried by an orphan boy.

The last of all the Bards was he,
Who sung of Border chivalry;
For, welladay! their date was fled,
His tuneful brethren all were dead;
And he, neglected and oppressed,
Wished to be with them, and at rest.

No more on prancing palfrey borne,
He carolled, light as lark at morn;
No longer courted and caressed,
High placed in hall, a welcome guest,
He poured, to lord and lady gay
The unpremeditated lay:
Old times were changed, old manners gone;
A stranger filled the Stuarts' throne;
The bigots of the iron time
Had called his harmless art a crime.
A wandering Harper, scorned and poor,
He begged his bread from door to door,
And tuned, to please a peasant's ear,
The harp, a king had loved to hear.

He passed where Newark's stately tower
Looks out from Yarrow's birchen bower:
The Minstrel gazed with wistful eye —
No humbler resting-place was nigh;
With hesitating step at last,
The embattled portal arch he passed,
Whose ponderous grate and massy bar
Had oft rolled back the tide of war,
But never closed the iron door
Against the desolate and poor.

The Duchess marked his weary pace,
His timid mien, and reverend face,
And bade her page the menials tell,
That they should tend the old man well:
For she had known adversity,
Though born in such a high degree;
In pride of power, in beauty's bloom,
Had wept o'er Monmouth's bloody tomb!

When kindness had his wants supplied,
And the old man was gratified,
Began to rise his minstrel pride:
And he began to talk anon,
Of good Earl Francis, dead and gone,
And of Earl Walter, rest him, God!
A braver ne'er to battle rode;
And how full many a tale he knew
Of the old warriors of Buccleuch.

— FLODDEN'S FATAL FIELD —

from *Marmion*

¶ *Marmion, an ignoble English knight tangled in a discreditable love affair, dies fighting against the Scots at Flodden. Defeat there in 1513 was one of the greatest disasters in Scotland's history.*

> But as they left the darkening heath,
> More desperate grew the strife of death.
> The English shafts in vollies hailed,
> In headlong charge their horse assailed;
> Front, flank, and rear, the squadrons sweep
> To break the Scottish circle deep,
> That fought around their King.
> But yet, though thick the shafts as snow,
> Though charging knights like whirlwinds go,
> Though bill-men ply the ghastly blow,
> Unbroken was the ring;
> The stubborn spear-men still made good
> Their dark impenetrable wood,
> Each stepping where his comrade stood,
> The instant that he fell.

No thought was there of dastard flight;
Linked in the serried phalanx tight,
Groom fought like noble, squire like knight,
As fearlessly and well;
Till utter darkness closed her wing
O'er their thin host and wounded King.
Then skilful Surrey's sage commands
Led back from strife his shattered bands;
And from the charge they drew,
As mountain-waves, from wasted lands,
Sweep back to ocean blue.
Then did their loss his foemen know;
Their King, their Lords, their mightiest low,
They melted from the field as snow,
When streams are swoln and south winds blow,
Dissolves in silent dew.
Tweed's echoes heard the ceaseless plash,
While many a broken band,
Disordered, through her currents dash,
To gain the Scottish land;
To town and tower, to down and dale,
To tell red Flodden's dismal tale,
And raise the universal wail.

Tradition, legend, tune, and song,
Shall many an age that wail prolong:
Still from the sire the son shall hear
Of the stern strife, and carnage drear,
Of Flodden's fatal field,
Where shivered was fair Scotland's spear
And broken was her shield!

— THE STAG HUNT —

from *The Lady of the Lake*

❡ *In the poem James V of Scotland, incognito until near the end, gets lost during the hunt described below, falls in love with Ellen, 'the Lady of the Lake', fights with the Highland chieftain Roderick Dhu and chivalrously yields Ellen to her lover, Malcolm Graeme.*

The Stag at eve had drunk his fill,
Where danced the moon on Monan's rill,
And deep his midnight lair had made
In lone Glenartney's hazel shade;
But, when the sun his beacon red
Had kindled on Benvoirlich's head,
The deep-mouthed blood-hound's heavy bay
Resounded up the rocky way,
And faint, from farther distance borne,
Were heard the clanging hoof and horn.

As Chief who hears his warder call,
'To arms! the foemen storm the wall,'
The antlered monarch of the waste
Sprung from his heathery couch in haste.

But, ere his fleet career he took,
The dew-drops from his flanks he shook;
Like crested leader proud and high,
Tossed his beamed frontlet to the sky;
A moment gazed adown the dale,
A moment snuffed the tainted gale,
A moment listened to the cry,
That thickened as the chase drew nigh:
Then, as the headmost foes appeared,
With one brave bound the copse he cleared,
And, stretching forward free and far,
Sought the wild heaths of Uam-Var.

Yelled on the view the opening pack;
Rock glen and cavern paid them back;
To many a mingled sound at once
The awakened mountain gave response.
A hundred dogs bayed deep and strong,
Clattered a hundred steeds along,
Their peal the merry horns rung out,
A hundred voices joined the shout;
With hark and whoop and wild halloo,
No rest Benvoirlich's echoes knew.

Far from the tumult fled the roe,
Close in her covert cowered the doe;
The falcon, from her cairn on high,
Cast on the rout a wondering eye,
Till far beyond her piercing ken
The hurricane had swept the glen.
Faint, and more faint, its failing din
Returned from cavern, cliff, and linn,
And silence settled, wide and still,
On the lone wood and mighty hill.

Less loud the sounds of sylvan war
Disturbed the heights of Uam-Var,
And roused the cavern, where 'tis told
A giant made his den of old;
For ere that steep ascent was won,
High in his pathway hung the sun,
And many a gallant, stayed perforce,
Was fain to breath his faltering horse,
And of the trackers of the deer,
Scarce half the lessening pack was near;
So shrewdly, on the mountain side,
Had the bold burst their mettle tried.

The noble Stag was pausing now
Upon the mountain's southern brow,
Where broad extended, far beneath
The varied realms of fair Menteith.
With anxious eye he wandered o'er
Mountain and meadow, moss and moor,
And pondered refuge from his toil
By far Lochard or Aberfoyle.
But nearer was the copsewood gray,
That waved and wept on Loch Achray,
And mingled with the pine-trees blue
On the bold cliffs of Benvenue.
Fresh vigour with the hope returned,
With flying foot the heath he spurned,
Held westward with unwearied race,
And left behind the panting chase.

— THE EVE OF BANNOCKBURN —

from *The Lord of the Isles*

¶ *The love-story of Edith of Lorn and Ronald, Lord of the
Isles, is woven into the historical narrative of King Robert the
Bruce's victory over the English at Bannockburn in 1314. This
passage describes the Scottish monarch's narrow escape as he
reviews his troops the evening before the battle.*

> Armed all on foot, that host appears
> A serried mass of glimmering spears.
> There stood the Marchers' warlike band,
> The warriors there of Lodon's land;
> Ettrick and Liddell bent the yew,
> A band of archers fierce, though few:
> The men of Nith and Annan's vale,
> And the bold spears of Teviotdale —
> The dauntless Douglas these obey,
> And the young Stuart's gentle sway.
> North-eastward by Saint Ninian's shrine,
> Beneath fierce Randolph's charge, combine
> The warriors whom the hardy North
> From Tay to Sutherland sent forth.
> The rest of Scotland's war-array
> With Edward Bruce to westward lay,

Where Bannock, with his broken bank
And deep ravine, protects their flank.
Behind them, screened by sheltering wood,
The gallant Keith, Lord Marshal, stood:
His men-at-arms bear mace and lance,
And plumes that wave, and helms that glance.
Thus fair divided by the King,
Centre, and right, and leftward wing,
Composed his front; nor distant far
Was strong reserve to aid the war.
And 'twas to front of this array,
Her guide and Edith made their way.

Here must they pause; for, in advance
As far as one might pitch a lance,
The Monarch rode along the van,
The foe's approaching force to scan,
His line to marshal and to range,
And ranks to square, and fronts to change.
Alone he rode — from head to heel
Sheathed in his ready arms of steel;
Nor mounted yet on war-horse wight,   *strong*
But, till more near the shock of fight,
Reining a palfrey low and light.
A diadem of gold was set

Above his bright steel basinet,
And clasped within its glittering twine
Was seen the glove of Argentine;   *Sir Giles de Argentein*
Truncheon or leading staff he lacks,
Bearing, instead, a battle-axe.
He ranged his soldiers for the fight,
Accoutred thus, in open sight
Of either host. Three bowshots far,
Paused the deep front of England's war,
And rested on their arms awhile,
To close and rank their warlike file,
And hold high council, if that night
Should view the strife, or dawning light.

O gay, yet fearful to behold,
Flashing with steel and rough with gold,
And bristled o'er with bills and spears,
With plumes and pennons waving fair,
Was that bright battle-front! for there
Rode England's King and peers:
And who, that saw that Monarch ride,
His kingdom battled by his side,
Could then his direful doom foretell!
Fair was his seat in knightly selle,
And in his sprightly eye was set
Some spark of the Plantagenet.

Though light and wandering was his glance,
It flashed at sight of shield and lance.
'Know'st thou,' he said, 'De Argentine,
Yon knight who marshals thus their line?'
'The tokens on his helmet tell
The Bruce, my Liege: I know him well.'
'And shall the audacious traitor brave
The presence where our banners wave?'
'So please my Liege,' said Argentine,
'Were he but horsed on steed like mine,
To give him fair and knightly chance,
I would adventure forth my lance.'
'In battle-day,' the King replied,
'Nice tourney rules are set aside.
Still must the rebel dare our wrath?
Set on him, sweep him from our path!'
And, at King Edward's signal, soon
Dashed from the ranks Sir Henry Boune.

Of Hereford's high blood he came,
A race renowned for knightly fame.
He burned before his Monarch's eye
To do some deed of chivalry.
He spurred his steed, he couched his lance,
And darted on the Bruce at once.
As motionless as rocks, that bide

The wrath of the advancing tide,
The Bruce stood fast. Each breast beat high,
And dazzled was each gazing eye,
The heart had hardly time to think,
The eyelid scarce had time to wink,
While on the King, like flash of flame,
Spurred to full speed the war-horse came!
The partridge may the falcon mock
If that slight palfrey stand the shock;
But swerving from the Knight's career,
Just as they met, Bruce shunned the spear.
Onward the baffled warrior bore
His course — but soon his course was o'er!
High in his stirrups stood the King,
And gave his battle-axe the swing.
Right on De Boune, the whiles he passed,
Fell that stern dint, the first, the last!
Such strength upon the blow was put,
The helmet crashed like hazel-nut;
The axe-shaft, with its brazen clasp,
Was shivered to the gauntlet grasp.
Springs from the blow the startled horse,
Drops to the plain the lifeless corse;
First of that fatal field, how soon,
How sudden, fell the fierce De Boune!

One pitying glance the Monarch sped
Where on the field his foe lay dead;
Then gently turned his palfrey's head,
And, pacing back his sober way,
Slowly he gained his own array.
There round their King the leaders crowd,
And blame his recklessness aloud,
That risked 'gainst each adventurous spear
A life so valued and so dear.
His broken weapon's shaft surveyed
The King, and careless answer made,
'My loss may pay my folly's tax;
I've broke my trusty battle-axe.'

III

REMINISCENCES IN VERSE

The introductory epistles to the cantos of *Marmion*, each to a different friend, are full of affectionate reminiscence of happy times in the Borders at different seasons. They have nothing whatsoever to do with the tale of *Marmion* and indeed were at one time intended as a separate publication.

— THE END OF AUTUMN —

to William Stuart Rose

November's sky is chill and drear,
November's leaf is red and sear;
Late, gazing down the steepy linn,
That hems our little garden in,
Low in its dark and narrow glen,
You scarce the rivulet might ken,
So thick the tangled greenwood grew,
So feeble trilled the streamlet through:
Now murmuring hoarse, and frequent seen
Through bush and briar, no longer green,
An angry brook, it sweeps the glade,
Brawls over rock and wild cascade,
And, foaming brown with doubled speed,
Hurries its waters to the Tweed.

No longer Autumn's glowing red
Upon our Forest hills is shed;
No more, beneath the evening beam,
Fair Tweed reflects their purple gleam;
Away hath passed the heather-bell,
That bloomed so rich on Neidpath-fell;
Sallow his brow, and russet bare
Are now the sister-heights of Yair.

The sheep, before the pinching heaven,
To sheltered dale and down are driven,
Where yet some faded herbage pines,
And yet a watery sunbeam shines:
In meek despondency they eye
The withered sward and wintry sky,
And far beneath their summer hill,
Stray sadly by Glenkinnon's rill:
The shepherd shifts his mantle's fold,
And wraps him closer from the cold;
His dogs no merry circles wheel,
But shivering follow at his heel;
A cowering glance they often cast,
As deeper moans the gathering blast.

My imps, though hardy, bold, and wild,
As best befits the mountain child,
Feel the sad influence of the hour,
And wail the daisy's vanished flower;
Their summer gambols tell, and mourn,
And anxious ask, — Will spring return,
And birds and lambs again be gay,
And blossoms clothe the hawthorn spray?

Yes, prattlers, yes; the daisy's flower
Again shall paint your summer bower;
Again the hawthorn shall supply
The garlands you delight to tie;
The lambs upon the lea shall bound,
The wild birds carol to the round,
And, while you frolic light as they,
Too short shall seem the summer day.

— SMAILHOLM TOWER —

to William Erskine

¶ *Smailholm Tower, beside the farm where Scott spent many months with his grandparents as a boy, was the setting for 'The Eve of St John' (page 38 above).*

Thus, while I ape the measure wild
Of tales that charmed me yet a child,
Rude though they be, still with the chime
Return the thoughts of early time;
And feelings, roused in life's first day,
Glow in the line, and prompt the lay.
Then rise those crags, that mountain tower
Which charmed my fancy's wakening hour.
Though no broad river swept along,
To claim, perchance, heroic song;
Though sighed no groves in summer gale,
To prompt of love a softer tale;
Though scare a puny streamlet's speed
Claimed homage from a shepherd's reed;
Yet was poetic impulse given,
By the green hill and clear blue heaven.
It was a barren scene, and wild,
Where naked cliffs were rudely piled;
But ever and anon between

Lay velvet tufts of loveliest green;
And well the lonely infant knew
Recesses where the wall-flower grew,
And honeysuckle loved to crawl
Up the low crag and ruined wall.
I deemed such nooks the sweetest shade
The sun in all his round surveyed;
And still I thought that shattered tower
The mightiest work of human power;
And marvelled, as the aged hind
With some strange tale bewitched my mind,
Of forayers, who, with headlong force,
Down from that strength had spurred their horse,
Their southern rapine to renew,
Far in the distant Cheviots blue,
And, home returning, filled the hall
With revel, wassel-rout, and brawl.
Methought that still with tramp and clang
The gateway's broken arches rang;
Methought grim features, seamed with scars,
Glared through the windows' rusty bars.

And ever, by the winter hearth,
Old tales I heard of woe or mirth,
Of lovers' sleights, of ladies' charms,
Of witches' spells, of warriors' arms;

Of patriot battles, won of old
By Wallace wight and Bruce the bold;
Of later fields of feud and fight,
When, pouring from their Highland height,
The Scottish clans, in headlong sway,
Had swept the scarlet ranks away.
While stretched at length upon the floor,
Again I fought each combat o'er,
Pebbles and shells, in order laid,
The mimic ranks of war displayed;
And onward still the Scottish Lion bore,
And still the scattered Southron fled before.

Still, with vain fondness, could I trace,
Anew, each kind familiar face,
That brightened at our evening fire;
From the thatched mansion's grey-haired Sire,
Wise without learning, plain and good,
And sprung of Scotland's gentler blood;
Whose eye in age, quick, clear, and keen,
Showed what in youth its glance had been;
Whose doom discording neighbours sought,
Content with equity unbought;
To him the venerable Priest,
Our frequent and familiar guest,
Whose life and manners well could paint

Alike the student and the saint;
Alas! whose speech too oft I broke
With gambol rude and timeless joke:
For I was wayward, bold, and wild,
A self-willed imp, a grandame's child;
But half a plague, and half a jest,
Was still endured, beloved, caressed.

From me, thus nurtured, dost thou ask
The classic poet's well-conned task?
Nay, Erskine, nay — on the wild hill
Let the wild heathbell flourish still;
Cherish the tulip, prune the vine,
But freely let the woodbine twine,
And leave untrimmed the eglantine:
Nay, my friend, nay — since oft thy praise
Hath given fresh vigour to my lays,
Since oft thy judgment could refine
My flattened thought, or cumbrous line,
Still kind, as is thy wont, attend,
And in the minstrel spare the friend.
Though wild as cloud, as stream, as gale,
Flow forth, flow unrestrained, my Tale!

— SUMMER RAMBLES —

to James Skene

To thee, perchance, this rambling strain
Recalls our summer walks again;
When, doing nought — and, to speak true,
Not anxious to find aught to do —
The wild unbounded hills we ranged,
While oft our talk its topic changed,
And, desultory as our way,
Ranged, unconfined, from grave to gay.
Even when it flagged, as oft will chance,
No effort made to break its trance,
We could right pleasantly pursue
Our sports in social silence too;
Thou gravely labouring to portray
The blighted oak's fantastic spray;
I spelling o'er with much delight,
The legend of that antique knight,
Tirante by name, ycleped the White.
At either's feet a trusty squire,
Pandour and Camp, with eyes of fire,
Jealous, each other's motions viewed,
And scarce suppressed their ancient feud.

The laverock whistled from the cloud;
The stream was lively, but not loud;
From the whitethorn the May-flower shed
Its dewy fragrance round our head;
Not Ariel lived more merrily
Under the blossomed bough than we.

— CHRISTMAS —

to Richard Heber

Heap on more wood! — the wind is chill;
But let it whistle as it will,
We'll keep our Christmas merry still.
Each age has deemed the new-born year
The fittest time for festal cheer:
Even, heathen yet, the savage Dane
At Iol more deep the mead did drain;   *Yule*
High on the beach his galleys drew,
And feasted all his pirate crew;
Then in his low and pine-built hall,
Where shields and axes decked the wall,
They gorged upon the half-dressed steer;
Caroused in seas of sable beer;
While round, in brutal jest, were thrown
The half-gnawed rib, and marrow-bone:
Or listened all, in grim delight,
While Scalds yelled out the joys of fight,
Then forth, in frenzy, would they hie,
While wildly-loose their red locks fly,
And dancing round the blazing pile,
They make such barbarous mirth the while,
As best might to the mind recall
The boisterous joys of Odin's hall.

And well our Christian sires of old
Loved when the year its course had rolled,
And brought blithe Christmas back again,
With all his hospitable train.
Domestic and religious rite
Gave honour to the holy night;
On Christmas Eve the bells were rung;
On Christmas Eve the mass was sung;
The only night in all the year,
Saw the stoled priest the chalice rear.
The damsel donned her kirtle sheen;   *gorgeous g*
The hall was dressed with holly green;
Forth to the wood did merry-men go,
To gather in the mistletoe.
Then opened wide the Baron's hall
To vassal, tenant, serf and all;
Power laid his rod of rule aside
And Ceremony doffed his pride.
The heir, with roses in his shoes,
That night might village partner choose;
The Lord, underogating, share
The vulgar game of 'post and pair'.
All hailed, with uncontrolled delight,
And general voice, the happy night,
That to the cottage, as the crown,
Brought tidings of salvation down.

The fire, with well-dried logs supplied,
Went roaring up the chimney wide;
The huge hall-table's oaken face,
Scrubbed till it shone, the day to grace,
Bore then upon its massive board
No mark to part the squire and lord.
Then was brought in the lusty brawn,
By the old blue-coated serving-man;
Then the grim boar's head frowned on high,
Crested with bays and rosemary.
Well can the green-garbed ranger tell,
How, when, and where, the monster fell;
What dogs before his death he tore,
And all the baiting of the boar.
The wassell round, in good brown bowls, *spiced ale*
Garnished with ribbons, blithely trowls.
There the huge sirloin reeked; hard by
Plum-porridge stood, and Christmas pie;
Nor failed old Scotland to produce,
At such high tide, her savoury goose.
Then came the merry maskers in,
And carols roared with blithesome din;
If unmelodious was the song,
It was a hearty note, and strong.
Who lists may in their mumming see
Traces of ancient mystery;

White shirts supplied the masquerade,
And smutted cheeks the visors made;
But, O! what maskers, richly dight,
Can boast of bosoms half so light!
England was merry England, when
Old Christmas brought his sports again.
'Twas Christmas broached the mightiest ale;
'Twas Christmas told the merriest tale;
A Christmas gambol oft could cheer
The poor man's heart through half the year.

Still linger, in our northern clime,
Some remnants of the good old time;
And still, within our valleys here,
We hold the kindred title dear,
Even when, perchance, its far-fetched claim
To Southron ear sounds empty name;
For course of blood, our proverbs deem,
Is warmer than the mountain-stream.
And thus, my Christmas still I hold
Where my great-grandsire came of old,   *'Beardie'*
With amber beard, and flaxen hair,
And reverend apostolic air —
The feast and holy-tide to share,
And mix sobriety with wine,
And honest mirth with thoughts divine:

[96]

Small thought was his, in after time
E'er to be hitched into a rhyme.
The simple sire could only boast
That he was loyal to his cost;
The banished race of kings revered,
And lost his land, — but kept his beard.

VERSES ON SCOTLAND

The short passages on Scotland and the Border country which follow, all from the longer narrative poems, reflect Scott's passionate affection for the Scotland which his poems and novels were making familiar for the first time to the rest of the world.

The ruins of Melrose Abbey are only three miles from Abbotsford but Scott joked that he could not recall ever seeing them by moonlight. Norham is on the English bank of the Tweed, not far from the battlefield of Flodden. The impressive ruins of Tantallon Castle stand on the cliffs above North Berwick in East Lothian, close to the Lammermuir Hills. Edinburgh in *Marmion* is seen from the south side where the Scottish army was assembling to march towards England. Loch Katrine, west of Stirling, is now part of the Trossachs and Loch Lomond National Park. Two pleasure craft cruise Loch Katrine: the *Lady of the Lake* and the steamship, the *Sir Walter Scott*.

— O CALEDONIA —

from *The Lay of the Last Minstrel*

Breathes there the man, with soul so dead,
Who never to himself hath said,
This is my own, my native land!
Whose heart hath ne'er within him burned,
As home his footsteps he hath turned,
From wandering on a foreign strand!
If such there breathe, go, mark him well;
For him no Minstrel raptures swell;
High though his titles, proud his name,
Boundless his wealth as wish can claim;
Despite those titles, power and pelf,
The wretch, concentred all in self,
Living, shall forfeit fair renown,
And doubly dying, shall go down
To the vile dust, from whence he sprung,
Unwept, unhonoured, and unsung.

O Caledonia, stern and wild,
Meet nurse for a poetic child!
Land of brown heath and shaggy wood,
Land of the mountain and the flood,
Land of my Sires! What mortal hand
Can e'er untie the filial band,
That knits me to thy rugged strand!

Still as I view each well known scene,
Think what is now, and what hath been,
Seems as, to me, of all bereft,
Sole friends thy woods and streams were left;
And thus I love them better still,
Even in extremity of ill.
By Yarrow's stream still let me stray,
Though none should guide my feeble way;
Still feel the breeze down Ettrick break,
Although it chill my withered cheek;
Still lay my head by Teviot stone,
Though there forgotten and alone,
The Bard may draw his parting groan.

— MELROSE —

from *The Lay of the Last Minstrel*

If thou would'st view fair Melrose aright,
Go visit it by the pale moonlight;
For the gay beams of lightsome day
Gild, but to flout, the ruins grey.
When the broken arches are black in night,
And each shafted oriel glimmers white;
When the cold light's uncertain shower
Streams on the ruined central tower;
When buttress and buttress, alternately,
Seem framed of ebon and ivory;
When silver edges the imagery,
And the scrolls that teach thee to live and die;
When distant Tweed is heard to rave,
And the owlet to hoot o'er the dead man's grave;
Then go — but go alone the while —
Then view St David's ruined pile;
And, home returning, soothly swear,
Was never scene so sad and fair!

— NORHAM —

from *Marmion*

Day set on Norham's castled steep,
And Tweed's fair river, broad and deep,
And Cheviot's mountains lone:
The battled towers, the donjon keep,
The loop-hole grates, where captives weep,
The flanking walls that round it sweep,
In yellow lustre shone.
The warriors on the turrets high,
Moving athwart the evening sky,
Seemed forms of giant height:
Their armour, as it caught the rays,
Flashed back again the western blaze,
In lines of dazzling light.

— TANTALLON —

from *Marmion*

But scant three miles the band had rode,
When o'er a height they passed,
And, sudden, close before them showed
His towers, Tantallon vast;
Broad, massive, high, and stretching far,
And held impregnable in war.
On a projecting rock they rose,
And round three sides the ocean flows,
The fourth did battled walls enclose,
And double mound and fosse.
By narrow drawbridge, outworks strong,
Through studded gates, an entrance long,
To the main court they cross.
It was a wide and stately square:
Around were lodgings, fit and fair,
And towers of various form,
Which on the court projected far,
And broke its lines quadrangular.
Here was square keep, there turret high,
Or pinnacle that sought the sky,
Whence oft the Warder could descry
The gathering ocean-storm.

* * * * *

I said, Tantallon's dizzy steep
Hung o'er the margin of the deep.
Many a rude tower and rampart there
Repelled the insult of the air,
Which, when the tempest vexed the sky,
Half breeze, half spray, came whistling by.
Above the rest, a turret square
Did o'er its Gothic entrance bear,
Of sculpture rude, a stony shield;
The Bloody Heart was in the field,
And in the chief three mullets stood,
The cognizance of Douglas blood.
The turret held a narrow stair,
Which, mounted, gave you access where
A parapet's embattled row
Did seaward round the castle go.
Sometimes in dizzy steps descending,
Sometimes in narrow circuit bending,
Sometimes in platform broad extending,
Its varying circle did combine
Bulwark, and bartizan, and line,
And bastion, tower, and vantage-coign;

Above the booming ocean leant
The far projecting battlement;
The billows burst, in ceaseless flow,
Upon the precipice below.
Where'er Tantallon faced the land,
Gate-works and walls were strongly manned;
No need upon the sea-girt side;
The steepy rock, and frantic tide,
Approach of human step denied;
And thus these lines, and ramparts rude,
Were left in deepest solitude.

— EDINBURGH —

from *Marmion*

Still on the spot Lord Marmion stayed,
For fairer scene he ne'er surveyed.
When sated with the martial show
That peopled all the plain below,
The wandering eye could o'er it go,
And mark the distant city glow
With gloomy splendour red;
For on the smoke-wreaths, huge and slow,
That round her sable turrets flow,
The morning beams were shed,
And tinged them with a lustre proud,
Like that which streaks a thunder-cloud.
Such dusky grandeur clothed the height,
Where the huge Castle holds its state
And all the steep slope down,
Whose ridgy back heaves to the sky,
Piled deep and massy, close and high,
Mine own romantic town!
But northward far, with purer blaze,
On Ochil mountains fell the rays,
And as each heathy top they kissed,
It gleamed a purple amethyst.

Yonder the shores of Fife you saw;
Here Preston Bay, and Berwick Law:
And, broad between them rolled,
The gallant Frith the eye might note,
Whose islands on its bosom float,
Like emeralds chased in gold.
Fitz-Eustace' heart felt closely pent;
As if to give his rapture vent,
The spur he to his charger lent,
And raised his bridle hand,
And, making demi-volte in air,
Cried, 'Where's the coward that would not dare
To fight for such a land!'

— LOCH KATRINE —

from *The Lady of the Lake*

And now, to issue from the glen,
No pathway meets the wanderer's ken,
Unless he climb, with footing nice,
A far projecting precipice.
The broom's tough roots his ladder made,
The hazel saplings lent their aid;
And thus an airy point he won,
Where, gleaming with the setting sun,
One burnished sheet of living gold,
Loch Katrine lay beneath him rolled;
In all her length far winding lay,
With promontory, creek, and bay,
And islands that, empurpled bright,
Floated amid the livelier light;
And mountains, that like giants stand,
To sentinel enchanted land.
High on the south, huge Benvenue
Down to the lake in masses threw
Crags, knolls, and mounds, confusedly hurled,
The fragments of an earlier world;
A wildering forest feathered o'er
His ruined sides and summit hoar,
While on the north, through middle air,
Ben-an heaved high his forehead bare.

VERSE FROM THE NOVELS

Songs and poems are scattered through the twenty-six novels which, after the publication of *Waverley*, became Scott's main literary preoccupation. Some are used as chapter-headings. Most of the verses in the novels themselves were written for a particular character or a particular moment; they therefore reflect the speaker and the speaker's view of life, not necessarily Scott's. It is Claverhouse who believes 'one crowded hour of glorious life is worth an age without a name,' and Lucy Ashton, not the author, who hopes to 'quiet live and easy die'.

— THE SPINDLE SONG —

from *Guy Mannering*

¶ *Meg Merrilies the gypsy sings 'what seemed to be a charm' while she spins black, white and grey wool with her distaff and spindle. For a new-born baby she prophesies fortunes as mixed as her wools.*

> Twist ye, twine ye! even so
>   Mingle shades of joy and woe,
> Hope, and fear, and peace, and strife,
>   In the thread of human life.
>
> While the mystic twist is spinning,
>   And the infant's life beginning,
> Dimly seen through twilight bending,
>   Lo, what varied shapes attending!
>
> Passions wild, and follies vain,
>   Pleasures soon exchanged for pain;
> Doubt, and jealousy, and fear,
>   In the magic dance appear.
>
> Now they wax, and now they dwindle,
>   Whirling with the whirling spindle.
> Twist ye, twine ye! Even so
>   Mingle human bliss and woe.

— SOUND, SOUND THE CLARION —
from *Old Mortality*

⁋ These four lines at the head of a chapter about James Graham of Claverhouse, were made famous by Scott but were actually written by Thomas Mordaunt.

Sound, sound the clarion, fill the fife,
    Throughout the sensual world proclaim:
One crowded hour of glorious life
    Is worth an age without a name.

— LUCY ASHTON'S SONG —

from *The Bride of Lammermoor*

¶ *Sung by the doomed bride of the novel.*

Look not thou on beauty's charming;
    Sit thou still when kings are arming;
Taste not when the wine-cup glistens;
    Speak not when the people listens;
Stop thine ear against the singer;
    From the red gold keep thy finger;
Vacant heart and hand and eye,
    Easy live and quiet die.

— PROUD MAISIE —

from *The Heart of Mid-Lothian*

❡ *Madge Wildfire, the wandering madwoman, sings (like Ophelia) 'wild snatches of songs and obsolete airs'. 'Proud Maisie' is the last of them, sung in her dying moments.*

Proud Maisie is in the wood,
    Walking so early;
Sweet Robin sits on the bush,
    Singing so rarely.

'Tell me, thou bonny bird,
    When shall I marry me?'
'When six braw gentlemen
    Kirkward shall carry ye.'

'Who makes the bridal bed,
    Birdie, say truly?'
'The grey-headed sexton
    That delves the grave duly.

'The glow-worm o'er grave and stone
    Shall light thee steady;
The owl from the steeple sing
    Welcome, proud lady!'

— COUNTY GUY —

from *Quentin Durward*

¶ *The hero overhears a beautiful stranger singing to her lute*
'exactly such an air as we are accustomed to suppose flowed
from the lips of the high-born dames of chivalry, when knights
and troubadours listened and languished'.

Ah! County Guy, the hour is nigh
    The sun has left the lea,
The orange-flower perfumes the bower,
    The breeze is on the sea.
The lark, his lay who trilled all day,
    Sits hushed his partner nigh;
Breeze, bird, and flower confess the hour,
    But where is County Guy?

The village maid steals through the shade
  · Her shepherd's suit to hear;
To Beauty shy, by lattice high,
    Sings high-born Cavalier.
The star of Love, all stars above,
    Now reigns o'er earth and sky,
And high and low the influence know —
    But where is County Guy?

VI

PERSONAL VERSES

The ups and downs of the romantic relationships of Scott's early life inspired these poems, which were not intended for publication.

— THE PRISONER'S COMPLAINT —

¶ *When he was seventeen Scott fell for the blue-eyed daughter of a tradesman in Kelso. When she came to Edinburgh for some months to nurse a sick aunt, he visited her surreptitiously, often having to hide in a closet until the old lady fell asleep.*

Come Jessie I impatient grow —
   Come hither quick I pray —
With meikle speed unlock the door,
   I can no longer stay.

The minutes into hours have grown
   Whilst I impatient wait,
E'en your old aunt would pity have
   On my unhappy state.

I came in hopes of welcome looks
   And words more welcome still;
I'm shut up in a gloomy hole
   And can't do as I will.

Instead of loving words from you,
   No sort of sound I hear
Save an old woman's sighs and groans
   That make my stomach queer.

Though tired of standing all this time
    I dare na stir a leg,
Though wishing sair to stretch my arms
    I canna move a peg.

The glasses tremble at my breath
    So close to me they stand,
Whilst jars are pressing 'gainst my feet
    And jugs at either hand.

Haste to prevent the threatening harm
    Or your old aunt I fear,
When glass and china fall and crash,
    Will think the devil's here.

Here's haddocks dry and barley meal
    And marmalade and jam,
And high suspended by a hook
    Above me hangs a ham.

But mid such heap of fish and flesh
    I uncontented live:
I hunger after fresher food
    Which you alone can give.

Untouched the tempting honey pots
    Upon their shelves remain,
For that I taste upon your lips
    Makes me all else disdain.

Come hither! You my closet are
    Where all my sweets are stored,
Oh save me from your aunt's good things
    And some of yours afford.

— THE VIOLET —

¶ *In 1786 Scott's heart was broken by the announcement that William Forbes was to marry Williamina Belsches whom Scott was also courting. Her marriage to Forbes was probably a love-match and was certainly approved by her parents, but Scott had deluded himself into thinking that he was the favoured suitor and that he had been jilted. Late in life he confessed that his passion for Williamina had been his one real experience of 'love in all its fervour'.*

The violet in her greenwood bower,
Where birchen boughs with hazels mingle,
May boast itself the fairest flower
In glen or copse or forest dingle.

Though fair her gems of azure hue
Beneath the dewdrop's weight reclining,
I've seen an eye of lovelier blue
More sweet through watery lustre shining.

The summer sun that dew shall dry.
Ere yet the sun be past its morrow,
Nor longer in my false love's eye
Remained the tear of parting sorrow!

❡ *Scott presented these verses with some wildflowers to a young beauty in a party visiting Hadrian's Wall from Gilsland Spa. Exploring the north of England with a brother and a friend, Scott arrived at Gilsland to see an uncle and aunt, but left some weeks later head-over-heels in love — not with the girl of the flowers but with Charlotte Carpenter, another of the guests at the Spa, whom he married a few months later.*

> Take these flowers, which, purple waving,
> On the ruined rampart grew,
> Where, the sons of freedom braving,
> Rome's imperial standards flew.
>
> Warriors from the breach of danger
> Pluck no longer laurels there:
> They but yield the passing stranger
> Wildflower wreaths for beauty's hair.

— WOMAN —

❡ *Although not a separate personal poem, these lines from*
Marmion *were surely inspired by the first ten years of Scott's*
married life.

> O, woman! in our hours of ease,
> Uncertain, coy, and hard to please,
> And variable as the shade
> By the light quivering aspen made;
> When pain and anguish wring the brow,
> A ministering angel thou!

— EPILOGUE —

Scott and Wordsworth had been friends for a quarter of a century, and the poet and his daughter were among the last visitors to Abbotsford before Scott set off for Malta and Naples in 1831 in a vain quest for renewed health. Scott took his visitors up the Yarrow to Newark Castle. 'On our return in the afternoon', wrote Wordsworth, 'we had to cross the Tweed directly opposite Abbotsford. The wheels of our carriage grated upon the pebbles in the bed of the stream, that there flows somewhat rapidly; a rich but sad light of rather a purple than a golden hue was spread over the Eildon hills at that moment; and thinking it probable that it might be the last time Sir Walter would cross the stream, I was not a little moved, and expressed some of my feelings in the sonnet beginning — "A trouble, not of clouds, or weeping rain".'

A trouble, not of clouds, or weeping rain,

ON THE DEPARTURE OF SIR WALTER SCOTT FROM ABBOTSFORD, FOR NAPLES

Nor of the setting sun's pathetic light
Engendered, hangs o'er Eildon's triple height:
Spirits of Power, assembled there, complain
For kindred Power departing from their sight;
While Tweed, best pleased in chanting a blithe strain,
Saddens his voice again, and yet again.
Lift up your hearts, ye Mourners! For the might
Of the whole world's good wishes with him goes;
Blessings and prayers, in nobler retinue
Than sceptre king or laurelled conqueror knows
Follow this wondrous Potentate. Be true,
Ye winds of ocean, and the midland sea,
Wafting your Charge to soft Parthenope!

SCOTT'S LIFE

ALTER SCOTT WAS BORN IN Edinburgh, a lawyer's son, in 1771 and died at Abbotsford in 1832. As a boy he was brought up in Edinburgh and the Borders. Since he became both a Clerk of Session in the Edinburgh law-courts and the Sheriff of Selkirkshire he divided his time in later life, too, between Edinburgh and the Borders — from 1812 at Abbotsford, the house he built for himself near Melrose. He was happily married and had four children.

The publication of the long, romantic narrative poems, *The Lay of the Last Minstrel*, *Marmion* and *The Lady of the Lake*, brought him fame and fortune. After the success of *Waverley* in 1814 he wrote a further twenty-five novels, the best-sellers of their day. King George IV created him a Baronet, and made the first modern Royal Visit to Scotland under his guidance. In Europe and America, as well as in Britain, he was the greatest literary celebrity of the day.

The bankruptcy of Scott's printer and publisher in 1826 ruined him financially. He made the heroic decision to write off not just his own debts but also those incurred by both firms and devoted the last six years of his life to that purpose. Sales of the books he wrote in that time and of a collected edition of his novels raised half the amount needed, and the sale of his copyrights immediately after his death wiped out the remainder of the debt.

Scott's selfless courage in adversity further enhanced his reputation. The newspapers announcing his death were edged in black.